Own The Interview

An Invisible Advantage

Richard Light

For more information email: breckexec@gmail.com

ISBN (ebook): 979-8-89571-389-1
ISBN (paperback): 979-8-89571-388-4

Success Publications SAR
R7L Publishing

Introduction

Congratulations. You have purchased what is potentially the second shortest book on interviewing in existence, as far as I know.

This book is a re-write of *Killer Interviewing* in order to free it from the confines of Amazon Kindle Publishing. *Killer* is still available on Amazon. If you have a KindleUnlimited subscription, got get it.

As I said in Killer Interviewing, I don't have the time or the motivation for researching whether there are shorter books on the subject. If it is brought to my attention there is a shorter one, I will shorten this and Killer Interviewing. I make time for petty battles.

You have an interview coming up; this is no time to dink around with 200 pages. However, I will ramble on a bit in an attempt to convince you that this book was worth purchasing.

I started writing an exhaustive bible on the entire recruiting world for the candidate and the hiring manager but got bored. If I was bored by it, I can only imagine the pain it would have inflicted on the readers. Too Long/ Didn't Read [TL/DR] is real and should serve as real feedback to long-winded pedants.

This book is communicated somewhat in the way I have taught candidates to interview. All candidates come to me knowing how to interview. They know how *they* interview and unfortunately most of them, from the first job out of college to the senior level executive, can be pretty average at it.

Practically none of my candidates purposefully learn or study about verbal and non-verbal communication from an interpersonal scientific perspective. They know what worked for them in the past and build their ego investments upon that. They all know what works because they got a job using it and they can pinpoint why. Just ask them. Then ask them to define the single cause fallacy.

I once had to remain pleasant while listening to an HR person telling their out-of-work friends they need to know a list of corporate buzzwords, have a self-assured personal sales monologue ready, and have all of their ending questions pre-prepared. You're not getting any of that nonsense here. Bless her little HR heart.

Your interviews from now on should help you determine *if* you want the job and if you want to join a particular company. You'll get a head start in determining if you want to associate with those people for the amount they will pay you. Because we are no longer looking for a job. We are now evaluating our options. As a result of reading this book, you should become choosier. Optionality is a good buttress for confidence and personal power.

<u>Why am I a relative expert in interviewing?</u>

I will tell you. I have been an Executive Recruiter working worldwide for over 20 years. I can have a conversation with anyone. I have conversed with 3 panhandlers standing in the shade next to a fast-food drive-through as well as with the CEO of that fast food company. All four were interesting people.

I have had business/ recruiting conversations with people in

North America, Latin America, Western Asia, Southeast Asia, Europe, Russia and within the many former Soviet countries. Fortunately English still seems to be globally popular.

Some weird assignments from some weirder companies have come my way. There have been thousands of people sent on interviews. I prepped and over-prepped them to talk to my clients. Whichever candidate got the job came down to my client's perception of who fit best. They all had the skills to perform the job so the cultural and personal fit were mostly in play. It was feel-ality over reality because in reality they were all relatively equal. This is what is happening when you are having a successful conversation. Feel-ality. I should trademark that word. Consider it trademarked: Feel-ality™

You may have noticed I said "successful conversation" not "good interview." Almost everyone who goes on an initial interview reports back to me that everything went well. Then I speak to the Hiring Manager and find out how well it really went.

Most people are skillfully average at judging their own performance especially when decision-making is based on to how the other person felt. The interviewee needs feedback from mentors or fans or parents or someone who is trusted and honest. They won't get real feedback after an interview from anyone other than a recruiter who might tell them the truth. Forget about HR. As they say, they aren't human and they aren't a resource.

Feels are subjective. Nobody takes their mom or their mentor or a 3rd-party body language expert to sit in on an interview and give feedback except for criminal investigators.

A good conversation has certain elements

The first is an establishment of comfort and rapport and an exchange of ideas, experiences, opinions. This exchange does not mean a 50/50 split of time talking or words generated by the speaker; or worse, the interviewee speaking the majority of the time. This is generally what I need to correct in candidates. Too much talking...

The last element is the ending. A good conversation has to have a good ending. The end leaves questions to be answered and motivates future action.

Pleading for more time or stalling the end is a desperate attempt to continue the conversation. This is why you will learn how to end a conversation as well as how to manage it.

In my business I need happy candidates who may become clients or will at least call me back and refer people to me. This is real recruiting. Calling people. When you get an unsolicited call from recruiters, call them back and chat. You will be ahead of 90% of humans with jobs in the conversation skills.

You may not be interested in the job or know of anyone but try to be helpful. Give the recruiter a name of a former boss as a potential source for more candidates. Say something like, "Hey, call this person. He knows a lot of people." Or "My boss at so and so company is great. She knows everyone." You will be logged in the recruiter's database as a good contact, a helpful person, the person to be called in the future. You are increasing the probability that the recruiter will call you one day with your dream job. I don't believe in dream jobs. That's a different book for later.

Many recruiters keep databases chocked full of notes from conversations they had with candidates and hiring managers. But the world has changed and gotten so efficient at bombarding information that people seem like they are getting a little fed up. The world of recruiting is infected with spam, texts, notifications, and a random email plague. Oof, now AI. I think AI could make a lot of calls for me and set up a lot of conversations.

In our brave new world, everyone is a personal brand however most people are horrible at sales and marketing for one reason: they pitch but they don't listen. Think of the constant pitches on social media. Did you know you have been shaving wrong? You have been using the mega shave blade company's blades and that is wrong because I have made a new blade based on old-timey blades that are now cutting edge new. The hyper-humongous tiny hair slicing mega-corps don't want you to know about the conspiracy.

And now because you are watching Youtube and I have spent money on telling you how wrong you are, you are now feeling insecure that you are a controlled spending-slave in the palms of shaving corporations who only want your money. You must now break free of your enslavement from mega shave and use your money to buy my shaving system before it's too late.

This diatribe is similar to the verbal spewage I get from candidates explaining to me how unique they are and how that uniqueness will translate into wowing my client.

Back to the point: the vast majority of modern initial candidate identification is done automatically especially in the corporate post and pray sourcing model.

When I, and most of my recruiting colleagues, identify a candidate for a client, this person has almost always come through a referral. This is a pre-qualification that modern, automated candidate collection lacks. How you are getting to the interviewing stage is up to you. This book is about that stage not your mass marketing efforts but we will touch on it very briefly.

Resumes are important. They are the calling cards that get you on the stage. Here is my condensed version of resume prep. You need to show features and benefits from your chronological past that describe your competencies and show how you will add value to another company in the skill function you provide. That's it. Use numbers as much as possible. Numbers mean things. Narratives about your uniqueness without proof means nothing.

If you want to pay a professional to write this, fine. Go do it. I can attest that I read resumes like an Executive – scanned over quickly at best. The problems I need address usually screen out from the pages. Basically, I want to know what you did and how it translates into what my client needs. Substitute "my client" with "the company you spammed" for purposes of online posting through whichever spamming site you love.

By the way, LinkedIn is a repository of historical fiction. Everyone knows that. It also gives me a paper trail to investigate the fiction. Don't worry, Internal HR Recruiters don't do this. They don't have the time nor the paranoia of a real recruiter to worry about such trivialities as embellishments on LinkedIn or resumes.

<u>The obvious features that should be on your resume:</u>

You increased market share. You were internally promoted. You worked for good companies. Or maybe... You jumped jobs every year on the red flag train. I will guarantee that any candidate who has job-jumped will have a prepared speech explaining why and it won't have anything to do with them.

Ok, you spammed some company who posted a job. Did you add in the keywords their AI Chimp is looking for? You will never know. Don't beat yourself up about this. Just spam the life out of anyone and everyone looking for your services or something close enough.

Job Swipe right, right, right, right...... You can filter out the uglies later.

It's not personal. This is business.

You scored a match! Finally we are where this book was intended to begin.

<u>The Interview Is Set</u>

I am assuming from this point on that we are in a standard modern interview process based on a posted job and begins with an Internal Corporate Recruiting interviewer person. If you live in other parts of the world, this more than likely applies to you as well because process and "best practices" is code for easiest, cheapest, and most efficient at generating the biggest bang for the buck regardless of being the "best" practice.

Swipe right, right, right, right.....works on your end. It's your duty from this point on to not be ugly and to peal back the pretty veneer revealing potential ugly at the interviewing company.

Next up is how...

But first a short story.

I got a call from a VP level candidate who was interviewing with a non-client of mine. He wanted to *pick my brain* on some things. He told me he was interviewing for a new role, had an initial interview set with HR, and felt like he "finally had his speech down." Cringe.

"Had his speech down"... What speech?

He is a VP with good credentials. They asked him to interview. Why the speech? I asked him this question and he responded, "Because they are interviewing me."

And I responded, "At your level you should be interviewing them. Hell, at any level this should be a mutual conversation."

Your resume has hooked...now it's time to reel in the job without breaking the line.

This is where nuanced expertise begins. But wait!

There's something you need to internalize and frame your mindset on. Mindset...I am starting to hate that word.

But never mind that because your mindset is more important than internet mindset gurus mindsets about selling you systems for mindset.

There are things that are inside of everyone: honesty, confidence, congruence, competence, and fear among other things. Fear is where honesty, confidence, congruence, and sometimes even competence hit the wall.

It's the fear aspect that we are going to work on and maybe

arrogance which is the dishonest faking of competence and confidence.

The most off-putting vibe you will give an interviewer is from fear, arrogance, and necessity. Arrogance will get your 30-minute HR interview cut to 10. Fear and necessity will put your resume towards the bottom of the pile.

In your mind, you may need this job. Your chances of over-selling yourself because of this insecurity are high. Your neediness is telegraphed and shows up as insecurity. Behind that cheap suit and the overtightened tie you dusted off is someone who is about to have their car repossessed and needs this job now! Your body language is screaming negative mammalian limbic brain things to the limbic brain receptors of the interviewer and this Feel-ality™ is bad for you.

That is super unsexy.

<u>NEVER EVER, EVER, EVER NEED THE JOB!!!</u>

Even if you really need a job, you don't need *this* job.

This where touches of arrogance may lurk without the mindset of confidence. After a few interviews where you have prepped yourself to remember you are not necessitous, this anti-necessity mindset will become easier and congruent within you.

One thing about arrogant people is that they talk a lot. Seriously, a lot. Their verbal flood is an attempt to mask the subconscious truth that is more than likely displayed in their body language.

To be confident is a practiced thing. You will fail at this. At some point you will break from the plan I am about to teach you. Once you know the plan, you should understand where you broke and see it in hindsight. You will become better and serve, maybe for a moment, as your own mentor.

Your mindset from this day forward is "no neediness." Never. Ever.

You are there to have a conversation with the representatives of a company who need your skills in order for them to make money and therefore pay you for the time you are there making them money.

You are interviewing them as much as they are interviewing you. You are being compared to the other people who are your competition.

Are you following me? Don't be necessitous. Say that again in your head. *I am not necessitous.*

Good practice helps remove this necessitousness. Over time, it will go away. Taking control of the situation will help you interview with honesty and integrity. With a plan, you begin interviews on your terms, less stressed, and less outcome dependent.

Now for the tactics.

There are two you will use for every interview: **The Flip** and **The Exit**.

TACTIC ONE: THE FLIP

Let's assume you posted your resume to a job and have lined up the standard 30-minute pre-screen with an HR Recruiter. This underling may or may not have any idea what the job entails but is tasked with checking your pulse and getting a feel for your congruence. This person might have some questions for you that serve to eliminate you from further conversation. More than likely, these questions came from an exasperated Hiring Manager who has been served too many inaccurate resumes.

Do not underestimate this person. This conversation can be a major roadblock between you and a real department head decision-maker. We "say conversation" instead of "interview."

This is another mindset thing. From this day forward you will think of interviews as conversations. The word "interview" is now stricken from your vocabulary. You will tell your friends that you "have a conversation scheduled for tomorrow with so-and-so at such-and-such company." By virtue of buying this book you are one of my candidates now and the candidates I present have *conversations*.

For our purposes, you have 30 minutes to wow and converse with this person. This HR person is also being wowed with amazing stories of corporate greatness by your unknown competition. You have no control over this. You can only be you.

This conversation will probably take place on the phone or maybe video. There will be tactical suggestions for these scenarios later.

After the greetings and pleasantries, you will be asked a question. Maybe something canned and lazy like:

So, tell me about yourself...

Or: What makes you interested in this job?

Or: How does your prior experience fit this job?

Or the dreaded: What makes you the best candidate for this role?

This is a trap. IT'S A TRAP!

These questions serve to get you to eliminate yourself as much as they serve to validate you.

But here is the kicker, <u>you have already been validated.</u> Your resume and past work history validated you. The AI Keyword Sorting Chimp found you for them. *Maybe* this HR person actually read your resume. You should assume it was read.

Regardless, AI Chimp is a pro and knows what it's doing. You are already validated. Nobody wastes their time doing useless interviews with schmucks who can't at least appear on paper to be able to do the job.

<u>There is no reason to go into a self-validating sales pitch to reiterate what this person should already know.</u>

Remember the example of VP guy? This is what he was planning to do during his *finally got the speech down.*

Your job is to take the question, briefly answer it without run-on sentences, and flip it into a question for the interviewer.

Such as: "How do you think your experience will add value to our organization?"

"I read the job description. It looks interesting and challenging. It's similar to my current job. What were your impressions when you read my resume?"

See **The Flip**?

Now HR Person gets to talk. And they love talking! Everyone loves talking.

But nobody cares about HR Person. Your competition doesn't care. All they care about is the canned self-validation speech they have practiced in the mirror to fill up 30 minutes and maybe more. They are thinking if they could get a 30-minute interview to last 45 minutes they must be doing well. Let them think this.

Do not interrupt HR Person. Let HR Person talk. Let HR Person talk the entire interview by continuing to briefly answer and turn the question back on them. This is called conversing. This talking-talker will feed you with little tidbits you can briefly add your insight to and ask more questions to keep the ball in play.

Be good at listening.

Avoid asking HR Person a closed-ended question. Use open-ended that start with: what, where, why, how, to what extent...

This is simple. If the question you pose begins with a verb, it can be answered with a "yes" or a "no" and is closed-ended.

HR Person: Did you like the culture in your last job?

You: I really did (yes). What do you like most about the culture here?

The word "most" is great in this context.

Here's a tougher one:

HR Person: Why are you looking to leave your current company?

You: I am up in the air about leaving. I saw your posting and thought I should at least have a conversation about it. It looks interesting. What can you tell me about it beyond what was posted?

You might hit the dead end with this.

HR Person: It is all there in the posting.

You: What are the soft skills that work best for it? or What is the department like?

Now lean in a little and smile and try to stay friendly with nice appropriate eye contact. Be interested. Interested listeners lean in a little.

Let HR Person burn up the entire time talking. It's like playing tennis with a skillful Octogenarian. You send the ball over the net and they hit back a lob. You have plenty of time to decide how you are going to keep the ball in play. Nobody thinks you are cool doing a smash shot on a little old lady Tennis Pro.

You notice that HR Person has talked through the entire allotted time: 5 minutes for introductions, 20 minutes of talking and you are 25 minutes into a 30-minute interview.

Even if the interview is longer, such as an hour, keep the ball in play with open-ended questions built on HR Person's or Hiring Manger's desperate failing attempt to control the questioning and stick to a script. HR Person might not even notice. You are so different than the other candidates with their endless self-aggrandizing prattle that HR Person is completely and rapturously losing track of time.

Their will to talk about themselves and their experiences at such-and-such company is more than likely stronger than their ability to control the situation.

The irony of this is that they will consider you to be an amazing communicator. This is all about self-control over your insecurities which are trying to make you talk too much. It is a practiced skill. With each interview you will get better. Most of my candidates who use this notice a positive difference in the first attempt.

NOTE: STAY ENGAGED WITH THE PERSON TALKING.

You are interested in what this person is saying. Stay engaged and interested. This person is giving you opportunities to ask more questions.

Remember this: explained competence is never more highly regarded than demonstrated competence. You are demonstrating your competence in interpersonal interaction which is the underlying key component to every job beyond crunching numbers, pounding nails, dotting i's and crossing t's.

You can almost guarantee that your competition is explaining their competence like mad unless they have read this book.

Now what? The agreed upon conversation time is running out. You are getting close to phase two...

Remember one more thing about interviews. It is about them, not you. They are selling themselves on you without being told (by you) that you are amazing. Every other candidate is telling them why they are so awesome. Generally, when someone is explaining their awesomeness in anything, they are ignoring the needs of the listener. This is one of the reasons we use **The Flip**. We keep the interviewer talking. Hit the ball back.

However, do not ignore direct questions about your competency in the job. Ignoring questions is not **The Flip**. Answer them with confidence. These can also be flipped.

Example:

Hiring Manager: I see you managed a $20 million project. How did that go?

You: It went well. It stayed on budget, was done on time, and the client was happy. I just got a nice follow up email from them last week. How does this align with what you are looking for?

Hiring Manager: Really well. We always deliver for our customers. It's important...blah, blah, blah...

Notice the "How does this align..." not "Does this align..." You are getting the Hiring Managers to sell themselves on you and giving you valuable information about the company. Hiring you is becoming their idea.

It makes sense to check up on the company as you wait for the scheduled next step. After your conversation, use whatever means you have to quietly quantify and qualify them as much as you can. But now you have to get out of there gracefully.

Tactic Two: The Exit

This is where I get blank stares from candidates I am prepping to converse with my clients.

They know this next thing to be true but like all real truths it is in conflict with their reality and feel-ality™. Their reality is an illusion. Here it is...

You will end the interview.

The Interviewee will end the interview not the Interviewer.

Say what? No. Wait. What? No.

YES!

You will end it. There is no discussing this. You will do this and you will do it well. You are my candidate. Failing to do this makes you a bad team player on my candidate team.

Fortunately ending the conversation is very simple. You were given a time frame for the conversation even if you are in a potentially ambiguous time frame such as a lunch conversation which ends itself. The wait staff ends your lunch. Don't worry. Lunch interviews are rare and usually far down the path towards offer letter time. Nobody in their right mind is going to schedule a lunch interview with an unknown schmuck.

In the 30-minute example, while HR Person is still yapping away and having a great time doing so, you notice that ya'll are coming up on 25 minutes. When HR Person pauses, you insert something like this:

"Wow, this has been a great conversation. Thanks so much. I know we only have 30 minutes scheduled and you are busy. Why don't I let you go? Let me know the next steps."

HR Person: "It's been great. I really enjoyed this. I'll be in touch...blah, blah blah." The more HR Person is engaged in keeping you around to talk, the better you did or the more free time this person is trying to fill up. Your job is still to end it with a smile and a "we'll talk soon. Great to talk to you. Bye." or some other similar thing and hit disconnect.

You end the interview. Don't let HR Person or Hiring Manager or CEO or whoever it is end it. You are in complete control to end a conversation that had a pre-defined time frame.

On the phone there is the hard disconnect. If you are in-person, you will need to imply that the conversation is wrapped up using the same little speech above.

The only reason you would ignore this rule is because someone with power like a C-level explicitly told you to stick around or else. And you will because not only are you respectful of their time but you are also good at following orders.

This will happen very rarely. People are busy. What is more important is that you are busy and you are not necessitous.

You are respectful and respect people's time. You are a wonderful person. You are grateful for the time allotted to converse with them.

Your blathering, validating competition will have an awkward ending to their interviews. It won't go smoothly. Not you... You yank the bandaid and get on with the day.

. . .

This is a powerful move.

It takes cajones. And you have cajones grandes. Remember, this is all done with a smile and the implication that this is not the end. You have served the ball back to their side. If they have time flexibility, they will more than likely attempt to keep you around.

HR Person: "Hey. Before you go let me show you around."

Be gracious. "Ok, I have a few minutes." Let them drag you around and be introduced to people. At the end of this parade, they will more than likely take you to the door where you will shake hands and walk out triumphantly understanding what you just did.

You just demonstrated respect for their time as well as respect for their feelings on purpose. You deserve a little treat. Go get one.

This works with everyone in the company. It works in panel conversations. It works with the CEO. It works with the person who will ultimately become your boss.

You are doing **The Exit** on purpose. It is a tactic you have done before or mentally rehearsed enough to let it flow.

This tactic works exceptionally well especially when you have no idea who your competition is. Assume they are not doing this. Assume they have not read this book.

Even if your competition has read it, at least you are on an even playing field and whoever gets the job will probably come down to minuscule differences. If HR Person or Hiring Manager has read this, more than likely they will keep this to themselves.

Something to remember. You are ending the conversation calmly, respectfully, and graciously. If you get the feeling you are doing this as a function of control like it is psychologically magical, you are missing the point. By pointing out that you are respectful of the interviewer's time, you are allowing them to actually pull the plug on the interview. It becomes their idea *suggested* by you.

Conversation Details

Here are some details to lengthen this already exhaustingly long book.

On the phone:

When interviewing on the phone, find a quiet place where you can stand up and move around. Use your earbuds and try to keep your hands free. You want to be able to move around and gesture while talking. I swear this comes through space and time and is received better on the other end.

Be careful of your earbuds though. Those little buggers have strong microphones that pick up everything. If you are stomping around on a hard floor, the person on the other end will know.

On camera:

Seriously for the love of all that is holy wear real pants, no jammies, no commando, no shorts. Just dress like you normally would for a face-to-face conversation – not super formal but be dressed like you care. Just because a CEO/ founder thinks wearing a hoody and looking like he is more interested in curing a sophomore hang-over than looking decent does not translate into *everyone dress like the that guy.*

Be on time:

Do I have to say this? Being on time is being early. 10 minutes early is enough earliness. Start incorporating time management into your life and you will always be on time. Log into the video chat a few minutes early, test the camera and audio then mute both until needed. Get up and prowl around while you wait; dust some furniture or whatever. It's better than staring at the screen.

Get to the parking lot early and know that there will be traffic problems on the way there. Adapt.

Some Interviewing Weirdos You May Encounter:

The Verbal Pause Attack Narcissist (The VPAN)

This is the person who is waiting for a pause in a conversation to pounce and redirect it towards their favorite current topic which usually is themselves or something they think is important. You might experience this wing-nut in a group/ panel conversation. Do not alienate this annoying freak especially if a question is posed. Flip it.

The VPAN usually just wants to be acknowledged and wants to feel like they have contributed by spewing out something they think is funny, important to the conversation, or attention getting. If you experience the VPAN and this person seems to be dominating the conversation but not leading it, that could be leadership-problem-warning-bells going off.

The Moral Interrogator (The MI)

I once had this dork of a human ask me what he phrased as *the most important question he asks all people* interviewing with him: "Have you ever lied?"

If you remember way back in the book, this is a close-ended question: yes or no. This is a question no one can answer well. The truth is that everyone lies. This is an automatic elimination question.

This type of question backs you into a moral corner. Everyone has lied at some point to someone. The question begs the question: does this guy have a history of hiring liars and is he reacting to his own poor decision-making by coming up with this ridiculous question? Maybe he's awful at evaluating people and is now overreacting. The reason you are backed into the corner is that you don't know what the context is. Context is important.

So I said, "You mean like if someone asks, 'Do I look great in these jeans?' Of course I have lied about that. If that's what you mean. What are some of the best lies you have been told?" See **The Flip**? He sort of scuffled around that question creating more worrisome questions for me.

The whole thing was off-putting for me for sure. I would place bets that he probably hired someone who lies to him. Moral posturing like this trains people to lie to you and bad managers deserve bad employees who lie to them.

The Flip method does a fantastic job of avoiding the classic mistake of telling people what you think they want to hear.

. . .

<u>The Standardized Test Interview-tard (The STIT)</u>

This is the interviewer who will make **The Flip** virtually impossible. This person is fixated on getting through a prefabricated list of disqualifying questions. Wait, say what?

You heard that right, *disqualifying questions*. Your hyper-positive, all is rainbows mystical dream-state thinks all questions are made to qualify you. With the STIT person your feels will tell you they are made to disqualify you.

This freak is intent on getting through the question list in the allotted time. Whatever your timeframe is, know that the STIT has subconsciously considered an allotted time for each of your answers. You will know if you are using too much because the STIT will non-verbally show distress such as a furrowed brow. This is not a conversation as much as an interrogation. And of course, I have a personal example.

I sat there near the end of the long conference table comfortably near HR Person but not too close as to imply "what are you doing around happy hour?" The VP of Operations walked in and waddled to the far end of the table separating himself from HR Person and me by 5 to 6 seats – strange. But not to worry I am awesome and I am going to flip this dude's brains out. At the end, we will be bros and he will get up and man-hug me. For tomorrow we will take to the field and conquer! Nope. He was a rabid STIT.

As he slouched in his chair, he stared down at his list of disqualifiers and fired them off one by one. All I could think of was, in this recruiting role I could replace this idiot first. I know hundreds of capable VPs of Operations who would be great to replace him. It is no surprise they have a chronic staffing problem in his department. How do I sell: "You are going to work for a sad sack of psychopathy," to everyone they want me to recruit?

Simple. I undermine this chump and replace him. Alas, I won't because watching a sinking ship sink is sort of fun especially when you know that everyone who is anyone is already on a lifeboat. I can't even remember the questions. All I can remember to this day is his droopy posture and how many people I knew who could replace him.

We finally got to the end of the interrogation when his remaining question was "do you have any questions?" And I did and it sealed my fate.

Me: "What do you think is broken in your system that creates so much turn-over?" As I sat back smugly waiting. My day-long-with-everyone interview suddenly ended because the CEO and CFO were called into an emergency meeting. Yeah, right.

Everybody lies. I saw this meeting taking place. They were hip and had one of those fish tank conference rooms where they can posture productivity. Apparently emergency meetings at this company entail a lot of laughter, smiles and catering not the stern, self-important performative crisis management I expected to see.

So, I did what I normally do when a company has a crappy employee they have put into a power position. I periodically sent a marketing email to the CEO about a potential replacement candidate for that role. It never amounts to anything but it is my dirty little 30-second high of vindictiveness that I yearn for from time to time. What can I say? Sometimes I am human.

Fortunately, these types of humans are somewhat rare. Most people are pretty nice and just want to get through a workday with nice people, keep their jobs, and advance themselves professionally.

The Flip and **The Exit** are good starting points in making new work allies. After you get the job, it's up to you to do the work, make the money, and seize the power.

One last thing on talking

The amount of words used (chatter) does not, in any way,

indicate the truth of what is being said. This is one of the reasons we keep the answers to an interviewer's question succinct and to the point. Long winded crap is still crap. Flipping questions back creates a conversation out of an interview. It demonstrates interest in the other person, the company and the job.

Remember this and remind yourself before you interview:

- I am validated by your resume
- I am not necessitous
- I have options

<u>You are there to have a conversation</u>

Flipping their questions opens the interviewer up to converse. If you find yourself stuck in a series of questions (an interrogation), look for a pause to work in an open ended question – a tactical adaptation of VPAN. It's best in a conversation to trading shots back and forth instead of getting yourself trapped on the defensive. Interrogator interviewing should be a major red flag about the job, the company, the interviewer, the department…

More than likely you have been interviewing in the standard form up until now – to validate and revalidate yourself. You will discover quickly that conversations get the interviewees to open up about the company and the role. Happy people are happy at work and at home. It is worth it to spend time with them.

You will gain more valuable information for future decision-making. Good interviewers enjoy these exchanges because everyone loves to talk to people who listen. You are unique because you're not there to give a 30-minute sales pitch on the resume they have already read. You're a real person. The interviewer is becoming comfortable with you from the start instead feeling adversarial.

When you leave an interview after using **The Flip** and **The Exit** especially with your potential new boss, I would put money on them picking up your resume and actually reading it. Their brain is saying, "I like that person. The person can do the job, right? Let's look for something wrong. There's something wrong and it's in this resume I scanned. Hum, nothing here. Maybe this is my new Director of Directing Something… I'll get some references., maybe do some snooping."

<u>Remember The Power move</u>

Begin using **The Exit** a few minutes before the allotted time-frame. This shows you are respectful of their time and your own.

Now go to your next interview and do the same thing – over and over and collect offer letters.

Remember, arrogance is fakery mimicking confidence. If you haven't perfected this technique in the first round, keep at it until you have internalized it. There are only two things to remember.

Eventually, after multiple interviews and offers, your confidence will project an aura of true competence. Competence comes from practicing something over and over until it is internalized and virtually automatic.

Congruence is an internalized harmony and unification of confidence and competence. This is where you are headed.

<u>Never let your guard down</u>

There is a tendency to let these tactics go when you are far along in the hiring process and believe you have won. This is snatching defeat from the jaws of victory.

In one case, a candidate let his guard down when the interviewer asked about expected salary requirements. This is the number one question to waffle on.

It seems as though being straightforward and giving a number is being honest and it is. However, many interviewers are looking for a reason to disqualify you not test your honesty. IT MIGHT BE A TRAP! Assume it is.

Don't give it to them.

Here is a good, canned answer:

"Obviously I want to be fairly compensated for the work and have growth potential. What are you thinking as far as a comp range budget for this role?"

Budget is a good word to throw in since it removes people from making a personal statement and makes the salary number seem like it is part of a fair and impersonal system which it is.

If the interviewer cannot give an answer, politely say something like: "Let me know when you know."

Or "I trust you to make a competitive offer when the time comes for that."

Or they may say:

"Our range is 100 to 130 for this role."

And you will say something like:

"That falls where I was thinking. When you are ready to make me the offer, I will be happy to look it over."

This is a really good time to get out of there. Politely use **The Exit**:

"I know you are busy. I enjoyed our meeting and I am looking forward to seeing the offer…"

. . .

Silly Things Governments Do For You

The political idea of forcing companies to post their salary ranges is shortsighted. Most companies know exactly what they want to pay, what they can pay, and how much they need to pay. If they don't, the candidate market will quickly tell them. Their posted salaries are just finagling around a bunch of well-meaning and clueless politicians who are trying to convince you that they are helping.

There are already market forces compelling companies to post their salaries because everyone else is.

If it is you and the company in direct conversation, you can be fairly assured that their posted salary does not have a lot of wiggle room. Executive Recruiters between you and the company are better equipped to raise a company's expectations. I have done it more times than I can remember.

Sometimes it makes sense to take a cut. This is also the best time to have an Executive Recruiter in the middle or have direct contact with key decision-makers in the company.

An extreme example akin to winning the lottery

A friend of mine went to a small company and took a massive pay cut. He went from $2ooK per year in salary to barely $100k. His wife was not that impressed.

However, he got pre-IPO stock. She still wasn't impressed.

After a Private Equity company bought out part of his accumulated shares he was sitting on about $5 million. Wife warmed up to this and became more impressed.

Then they went public. I estimate he has now made around $30 million on that pay cut. He won't tell me the exact number but I know it's huge. Wife is sufficiently impressed.

Don't get hung up on salary and what it means to your ability to service more consumer debt. There is no job where salary can numb the pain of a bad job and sleepless nights before the impending doom of a long commute.

Try to look at jobs as stepping stones, future potential, learning experiences, etc. NOT SALARY.

Current salary requirements are what you need now to cover for the decisions you have made in the past. Evaluate your decision-making while estimating your future potential when considering a job and its salary budget.

<u>A note for older job candidates</u>

I have heard this line too many times and it never works.

"At this point in my career, I am looking for a home where my vast experience can add value. Blah, blah blah."

While all of that is true, you are doing the one thing companies hate. You are making the job about you and your needs. You need a home where you can ride off into retirement. Your vast experience is probably fraught with old thinking and old ways of doing things. You probably do not adapt like you did in your 30s. This is manicured necessity and it is not attractive.

<u>One more example on The Flip before you're off to battle</u>

One of the candidates who was an original field tester of these tactics reported back after I asked about examples of flipping.

Here is the text string:

Me: dude (I call him dude). *what are some of the interview questions you have flipped?*

Such as:

So...what do you know about our company?

Where do you see yourself in 5 years?

Him: In a sales interview I flipped when the guy asked, "Why should I hire you/give me your pitch"

I told him maybe he shouldn't hire me. I might not be a good salesman if I'm expected to sell a service (his business) that I can't stand behind. How would you communicate that we stand by our product?"

I showed that I have standards. [The interviewer] spent the rest of the interview defending his business and praising my honesty, and I showed him that he answered his own question why he should pick me, because I won't bullshit him.

Me: holy [expletive]...that's awesome

you showed him...demonstrate don't explicate

Him: Learned from the best

Me: that is some righteous self control you showed

Him: Yeah lol I was almost insulted that he expected an explanation

Me: it's like...show me how you're a...

Him: Exactly!

It was insulting lol but maybe he didn't realize that

This candidate got the offer. He gets offers all the time for jobs he has never done. He is the best guinea-pig-test-critter I know out there using this method – a true master of the art.

It Works

Why Does This Work?

It is simple and easy to remember. Your resume has already qualified you and all of the competition who will be interviewed.

You probably have heard, "Just hire the person... Jobs can be learned." Wow. Amazing… Everyone hires *the person.*

Some jobs require you to actually know how to do something right out of the chute. You can be guaranteed that you are not the only one who knows how to do the thing that needs to be done. You and the rest of the people who know the thing will be weeded out before the interviewing starts. The company is always hiring *the person.*

It is your job to demonstrate that you are the person through empathy, listening, being assertive, being generous, being in control of yourself.

This interviewing method does all of that. It trains you to relax and be those qualities. Some of you might need to practice this method over and over before you can get out of your head and just be in the conversation. So practice it. Use some PTO and go on some interviews.

Practice, practice, practice this method until it is internalized. There are only two tactics to master: **The Flip** and **The Exit**.

This method is the culmination of years of listening to candidates tell me about their interviews. I have personally used it at a time in my life when I really needed a job. Remember *not being necessitous*? I had no money. I had less than no money. I had to mooch my way to the conversation.

After I flipped one of the interviewer's initial questions, my future boss sat there selling the job to me while I said virtually nothing about myself. I kept hitting the ball back to her side of the net.

She had my resume. It demonstrated that I could do the thing they wanted done.

I added a little here and there, fed off of her statements, and posed questions for her. This went on for 2 hours. That is when I had the epiphany that someone had to end this on a high note and that someone was me. **The Exit** was born.

They scheduled a 30-minute meeting with her boss, the Regional Managing Director. He was a good guy. He said to me, "I talked to [her]. Your interview went well. You certainly can do the job, she really sold me on you already... What do you like to do outside of work."

I gave very brief synopsis of stuff I was currently doing then asked, "So, what do you like to do?" He talked for 20 minutes.

At 25 minutes in I looked at him and said, "I know you are really busy and we only had 30 minutes scheduled, I'll let you get back to work. Let me know what you want to do next."

He stalled my exit by taking me around to meet the team then across the building to show me a new space he wanted to move into. I looked for as many graceful exits as I could and eventually he released me from the verbal headlock he had on me.

I got in the elevator and laughed. That guy didn't know

anything about me. I barely said anything. I knew more about him than he did about me. Who was interviewing who?

I was necessitous in that moment of time. I really needed a job. However, I never communicated this verbally or non-verbally even though I was losing weight due to cutting back on calories. I should have been begging for this job.

I needed the job but I stuck to the tactics. It was in its infancy but had already served some of my candidates well. I get calls all the time from Execs who are moving from one company to another. I tell them this method and after a long thoughtful pause, they respond: "I get it. I see why that works."

This is not dark triad manipulation

This method combats your insecurities and penchant for over-talking when you are trying to impress someone. It forces you to be more human and a better listener. I used to think that I was tricking people into talking but in reality I was allowing them to talk by shutting up for once. No one has ever built rapport with someone by talking incessantly and unfortunately we all think of interviews as our time to talk about ourselves.

The first rule of recruiting is that everyone is lying to you

Every interviewer instinctually knows this. If they are doing most of the talking, who is doing the lying? Probably not HR Person. What would be the point of that? Since you are having a nice conversation and HR Person or Hiring Manager is getting to know you, neither of you is lying – certainly not you. You are asking really good questions and keeping the conversation going by responding to the cues given to you by the interviewer. It's those other people who haven't read this book who might be lying.

We are evolved with the blessing and curse of language. The lion with his mane and roar and the peacock with his tail cannot pad their resumes then go into an interview to explain their benefits to a company.

Peacock: "Check out these tail feathers ladies."

Lion: "The wind in my mane looks pretty good right now. Rooaarrr!!!!! Awesome, right? Hire me or I'll eat you."

Most people don't completely pad their resumes with outright lies; they embellish somethings and remove anything that could be questionable. Then they put on the best interview show they remember working at least once in the past. Or worse, they get all caught in their heads about what they should say or should have said desperately looking for a way to interject a preplanned tidbit of information they think will seal the deal and get the job.

This method always works. You might not get the job but it wasn't because of this. There are silent factors for and against you in the world of recruiting employees. Start every new job with an open mind and opens eyes.

The Halo Effect wears off quickly. If the company did a great job at selling you a lemon of a job, use the method and quietly begin interviewing while the lemon is paying you. Everyone lies – even companies.

Wrap Up

This book is getting too long. You have interviews to get to. This is it... **The Flip** and **The Exit**.

It is simple in theory but you have to practice this. One of my guinea pigs who started doing this really took to it quickly because he relied on its simplicity and kept it that way. You only have two things to remember. The skill is to flip the questions back on the interviewer gently and with real interest. The flipped question is fed to you by the interviewer.

Your interview exists to show who you are. Your resume shows what you are.

The resume shows that you are someone who has done a job that thousands and thousands of other people are doing. Conversations are two-way, win-win interactions that most interviewers experience as one-way resume rehashes. You are there to show you are human and through **The Flip** you are indirectly showing the interviewer you care about their opinions and who they are.

The Exit shows you care about their time and signals your inner strength.

Both **The Flip** and **The Exit** start off your interactions with HR Person, Hiring Manager, the Execs, and the company in general demonstrating that you can connect with other people. The key to this is to get comfortable with it.

Practice, practice, practice. Use it at the bar with friends, with the opposite sex, your grandma, or your neighbor. You will get good at it.

Be interested in the conversation. If you use this method like an arrogant robot, you deserve your fate. If you find you are losing interest in the job because the answers coming back sound awful, you can simply tell HR Person.

Or... or... what do we do class? <u>We flip it!</u>

Maybe instead of:

"You know. I don't think this job quite fits me."

Ask, "[HR Person], how do you think this role would evolve for me?" There might be something lurking under the sheets of HR that might interest you more. You might get asked to apply for a different job that you didn't know about. Strange things happen when you stop selling yourself like a Used Lemon Dealer and start conversing.

On a final note, you are going to have to talk during the conversation. It is worth repeating that your **Flip** questions are fed to you by the person interviewing you. Do not go in with a bunch canned open-ended questions and start firing them off. That is not a **Flip**.

The key is for you to influence the interviewer to talk a lot and sell themselves on you. They will feel good about it. They might even apologize for talking so much. I have had that happen and it is really funny on the way home.

Interviewer: "OMG, I feel like I talked the whole time..."

Me: "No worries. Good conversation. We'll be in touch soon."

Interviewer standing by the door now: "Thank you! Great to meet you!"

Me: "You too. See ya."

This strategy is designed to form you into a more confident, less necessitous conversationalist in regard to interviewing for jobs. That's it. Not much more than that.

Doing this has improved all of my candidates' abilities to have successful interviews. It has also made choosing someone more difficult for the Hiring Managers.

In the first rule of recruiting, *everyone is lying to you,* it is important to remember that these are not blatant purposeful fabrications where the person is telling you a complete falsehood hoping you believe it. The lies are usually slight tweaks of truth in order to manipulate the actual truth in favor of the person's perceived social status, ability to do a job, level of empathy, reputation or whatever positive attribute that person wants to convey.

These "lies" are not absolute truths akin to "you look great in those jeans."

About Recruiters

Recruiting Industry Basics

It's important to understand the middle character between you and your corporate aspirations. There are basically two types of agency recruiters and they will go through all sorts of verbal combat to explain to you why their modus operandi is best for you. This is a lie. It is best for them.

The Contingency Recruiter

This lovely person gets "paid on performance." That's their pitch.

What this really means is that they are not paid unless they produce a candidate that the client company does not already have and the company hires that candidate. Their business model is a numbers game. The more job orders they juggle and toss resumes at the better chance they have at placing one.

When I started out I was a contingency recruiter working for a contingency firm. At the time, the ratio was around 15 to 1. I would work on 15 jobs to maybe place one candidate. The jobs were constantly being refreshed by new ones in order to keep the good "close to the money" jobs nice and hot. The cold ones were tossed aside. This ratio does not really illustrate the numbers game risk factor.

Here is sillier example:

If you want to shoot a duck during duck season, go out everyday and randomly shoot into the air over a pond. Eventually, maybe a duck will cross your path at the right time and you will shoot a duck. That is day-to-day-to-day-to-forever contingency recruiting.

The contingency recruiter never specifically knows why they miraculously placed a candidate over the competition or what went right or wrong with you as their candidate. Their general connections with the client companies and hiring managers are relatively shallow. Some recruiters, like myself, cultivated really good relationships with specific hiring managers.

It is good to note that there is, on average, a 25% (of first year base salary) cost the company has to pay the recruiter for placing you. Companies don't like paying it and would like to avoid paying it. They hire HR Person or Internal Recruiter Person to avoid paying it.

Contingency recruiters usually give a 90-day guarantee period when they place you. You will notice that they will do follow up calls with you for about that much time before ghosting you until you are useful to them again. You are a number. It is a numbers game. This applies also to the contract hire firms. They are basically contingency firms.

The Internal Recruiter

I have never been one of these so my knowledge is formed from infrequent conversations with them and frequently speaking about them with hiring managers. Unfortunately these are generally the people most candidates will experience in modern corporate recruiting. They mean well. They just are not really recruiters. They are order taking paper pushers.

Hiring managers far and wide lament to me that their own internal "recruiters" don't understand the jobs they are recruiting and seem like they aren't working on them. That's not too hard to get your head around. These poor souls are tasked with recruiting everything the company wants. How could they understand all of the roles or have the time?

When you post to their jobs online, chances are you will have your first conversation with these people. Any specific questions you get from them have been passed along by a hiring manager who is trying to help weed out the *can't-do's*.

You would think that AI Keyword Sorting Chimp living inside their applicant tracking system would sort out the best for their human overlords. You would think this because you are nice, modern and positive. You are sort of right.

Most of the time AI Keyword Sorting Chimp does pretty well as long as the candidates are using the right keywords. This is a bit like job roulette. Toss the resume ball on the spinning posting site and it lands on red or black and sometimes those weird green slots. This is where AI Keyword Sorting Chimp picks up the ball, licks it and decides whether or not landing on the right number made it taste like bananas. If it does, AI Keyword Sorting Chimp eagerly shows it to its recruiting overlords. Oo, oo, oo...got one! And you are in! You are scheduled for a conversation. Thanks Chimp!

From there it is all about the process of scheduling you to converse with various people or sending you the *Respectfully go away. We don't need people like you* email. This is also a numbers game that is highly automated but it is "best practices" a.k.a. "easiest practices" that most people can learn and doesn't cost much. You can bet that there was a red-nosed salesperson involved in promising the company incredible results and better candidates for using the candidate seeking system they were selling to High-Level HR Person. Now AI will be the scapegoat for failure.

I will pause now to kvetch about AI and recruiting. I have been putting some thought into this. I could use AI very effectively to make routine, first contacts with a lot of candidates. But after that, the candidates will be back in a *being processed* type scenario by essentially the same systems they had before. I can imagine the interrogations an AI Recruiting Monkey could do. It sounds nauseating. It sounds like a really good way to lose all control of your confidentiality when looking for a new job. It may be best to avoid companies that are too enamored with AI recruiting systems. How many robots do you want to experience before you find someone with a pulse?

Back to the original topic. Internal Recruiters don't have guarantee periods. If you are awful or you quit because the company, your boss or the job is awful, they just find another you. I wonder if there is any real backlash for bad hires. Once the candidate is passed on to Hiring Manager, it is their duty to interview and hire and then manage. Internal Recruiter Person is more insulated. Agency recruiters are always blamable.

Full Retained Recruiter

This is me and others like the huge publicly traded recruiting firms. We start searches for clients by first being paid a portion of the fee to even think about working on it. No initial payment, no candidates for you Client Person. The initial payment means we are all in this together.

These recruiters are, in my opinion, the real recruiters. We have a lot in common with sport agents looking for a pitcher or punter or whatever for a ball kicking, hitting, throwing team. We are out to make this team win by adding you, the candidate.

Therefore, we will only send your resume if you get through our screening. No AI Keyword Sorting Chimps or splatter-the-resumes-and-hope-one-sticks methodology. This is pure recruiting through contacts, referrals, and industry connections.

I think it this is the best method for finding the best and I have a list of placed candidates that I believe proves it. However, it is usually the most committed relationship a company and or Hiring Manager will have with a recruiter. Much of Corporate America dislikes a lot of commitment in most of their candidate sourcing. They love us at the more senior executive levels which, ironically, I think are easier to recruit.

I have a few clients who like this method so much they find ways to use me on searches within their company's system that disallows such a thing. It's call finagling the system. These are my favorite clients.

If you are working with a retained recruiter as a candidate, you will get better feedback. You will have longer, deeper conversations regarding the role and how it fits your life. You can be sure that there are maybe 3 or 4 other presented candidates who are also having these conversations.

The retained recruiter will probably tell you how many other people are interviewing. Why not? It doesn't matter to the retained recruiter which one of you gets the job. It matters to the relationship between the hiring manager and the recruiter first, then to you. That being said, we want you to be happy because we are nice like that. It's a relationship we are fostering not a transaction.

As you can probably guess, the guarantee period for placing you will be longer. I offer one year. I think that is standard for retained. If it's not, it should be.

<u>What does knowing this do for you?</u>

As a candidate, knowing the channel through which your resume flows towards the job is important. Knowing where you stand is important. AI Keyword Sorting Chimp doesn't care about you. It cares about keyword bananas and it is getting fed them constantly. Have low expectations in these types of recruits and post early and often. Post and forget. Post and forget. Avoid post and hope.

Ask the recruiters who contact you if they are contingency or retained. If they won't answer that, they are contingency or some verbal gymnastics version of contingency. A retained recruiter will tell you.

The retained recruiter will normally volunteer this information upfront. The contingency recruiter may go Machiavellian on you and half-truth their relationship with the company. Some take an engagement fee upfront. That's sort of like retained but is not retained. It's buying some of the recruiter's time while the company find ways to not pay the recruiter the rest of the fee. It's a mediocre level of relationship at best.

The retained recruiter takes over the search completely. All candidates found by the recruiter as well as any candidates sourced by the company will go through this retained recruiter.

It is important to know how your resume is being fed to a company where your future blissful career development will be nourished if for nothing else than to manage your feeble attempt at willing the future to meet your expectations. Also try various pagan rituals.

For the vegans try burning kale instead of chicken bones. Or leave the kale on a rock in the sun for up to 72 hours if you want to avoid adding to atmospheric carbon dioxide. I hear this is effective. Regardless of your mystical future-tweaking modality, ask the recruiter what their relationship with their client is and remember the first rule of recruiting: everybody lies.

· · ·

Returning to the point of this book

Putting yourself in more control of the conversation puts yourself at ease. Remember that you are there for a purpose and the interviewer is in the power seat. **The Flip** neutralizes some of this power and creates a freer, more open and honest interaction. It gives you a sense of power balance between you and Hiring Manager or HR Person. HM and HRP should notice this not as a loss of their power but as gaining comfort and rapport with you.

Go out and practice this. Have great conversations. It is simple and is easy to remember: **The Flip** and **The Exit**, just two things…

Acknowledgments

This book is the culmination of over two decades of listening to and advising business professionals in the art of interviewing. I started asking candidates to think of their interviews as conversations about 15 years ago when I switched to only retained searches. The reason for this was all of the candidates I put in front of a hiring manager to interview already had good jobs. The candidates were looking at a new role as an opportunity to advance. They were interviewing Hiring Manager and the opportunity as much as they were being interviewed.

I would say, "If you have some interest, just go and have a conversation with them. It doesn't matter to me either way and it will at least confirm for you if you want to pursue it."

Thanks to everyone who has helped me cut through the muck and simplify interviewing.

<u>To one of my former bosses</u>

You have no idea how much I enjoyed our initial conversation. To be honest, the job was awful. Water under the bridge. I would definitely interview with you again. You are sweet. You can carry a conversation with minimal prodding for hours. You are a wonderful, caring person. I have no regrets. Thanks for being highly receptive to **The Flip**. I should add that as I sat there listening to you talk, I wondered why you were not asking me the the one true question I thought you should, "Why on God's green earth would you want this job?" And that was because you could not stop talking. Bless your heart.

To my former boss' boss

Dude seriously, get back into playing in bands. You are a cool guy who seems like he is missing his artistic outlet. The way you spoke about your former band glory said all it needed to say in 20 minutes until I hit you with **The Exit**.

As much as you love Former Boss, she's not right for you and I believe her husband will attest to this.

To my octogenarian tennis partner from way back when

Thank you for the tennis metaphors. Your skills were amazing. Best doubles partner ever. May your soul be blessed forever.

And finally, to my guinea pigs

Go forth and conquer, my brothers and sisters. You have validated this method over and over. Every time you are interviewing you report back to me with multiple offers, great conversations with potentially great new companies and/ or more information than you ever would have gotten if you spent the interview talking the whole time. You keep proving the efficacy of this method.

To all of the Hiring Managers, Directors, VPs and Execs who I have spoken to over the years

You all made this method evolve through all of your interview feedback. Thank you. There is no way this would have evolved without you.

About the Author

Richard Light recruited for Global Fortune 100 companies for over 20 years. His approach was one-on-one with direct interaction between the hiring manager and the candidates. Most of the candidates he placed went on to grow within their companies rising up through the ranks of senior management. He has placed people throughout the world including the US, Latin America, Russia, Europe and Southeast Asia.

Clients relied on his direct approach and information gathering. Candidates relied on him to prepare them for their potential new opportunity.

Most recently, he has been seen wandering away from the corporate world to write fiction.

ALSO BY RICHARD LIGHT